SANTA CRUZ PUBLIC LIBRARIES
Santa Cruz, California

D0119118

spot

AWESOME NATURE

SEASONS

by K.C. Kelley

AMICUS

sun

flowers

Look for these
words and pictures
as you read.

leaves

ice

Spring

Summer

Every year has four seasons.
Let's explore them!

Fall

Winter

Seasons change as Earth moves around the sun.

flowers

Look at the blooming flowers.
Spring is in the air!

sun

Look at the shining sun.

Summer at the beach is fun!

The sun shines brightly.

leaves

Look at the leaves.
Leaves change color in the Fall.
They turn red,
orange, and brown.

Look at the ice.
It is melting!
Winter is ending.

ice

Look at the happy children.

Spring is here again!

sun

flowers

Did you find?

leaves

ice

spot

Amicus Readers and Amicus Ink are imprints of Amicus
P.O. Box 1329, Mankato, MN 56002
www.amicuspublishing.us

Copyright © 2018 Amicus.
International copyright reserved in all countries.
No part of this book may be reproduced in any form
without written permission from the publisher.

Library of Congress Cataloging-in-Publication Data

Names: Kelley, K. C., author.
Title: Seasons / by K.C. Kelley.
Description: Mankato, MN : Amicus, [2018] | Series: Spot.
  Awesome nature | "Spot is an imprint of Amicus."
Identifiers: LCCN 2017022323 (print) | LCCN 2017034350
  (ebook) | ISBN 9781681513256 (pdf) | ISBN 9781681512853
  (library binding : alk. paper) | ISBN 9781681522456 (pbk. :
  alk. paper)
Subjects: LCSH: Seasons--Juvenile literature. | Readers (Primary)
  | Vocabulary.
Classification: LCC QB637.4 (ebook) | LCC QB637.4 .K45 2018
  (print) | DDC 508.2--dc23
LC record available at https://lccn.loc.gov/2017022323

Printed in China
HC 10 9 8 7 6 5 4 3 2 1
PB 10 9 8 7 6 5 4 3 2 1

Megan Peterson, editor
Deb Miner, series designer
Patty Kelley, book designer
Producer/Photo Research:
Shoreline Publishing Group LLC

Photos:
Cover: Sandra Cunningham/
Dreamstime.com. Inside:
Dreamstime.com: Pavel
Gramatikov 1, Thaiview
2tl, Viorel Dudau 2tr,
Keneaster 2bl, Ivansmuk 2br,
Lenazajchikova 3, Halil I.
Inci 6, Martinmark 8, Lilkar
10, Evgeniya Tiplyashina 12,
Sam74100 14. Shutterstock:
Johan Swanepoel 4.